Dogs
Know
Best

Two Dogs' Training Guide for Humans

1st Edition

Angie Salisbury

Annibury

Copyright

Typeset & formatting by : Access Ideas, access.ideas@yahoo.com

Visit our website at:
http://petlifelessons.com or http://annibury.com to learn more.

Four Paws Up!
Praise for Dogs Know Best

"Love it!! What a sweet book. Great lessons and boy, the love just jumps off the pages!"

"This is a winner! Angie shares stories that so many can relate to. I'd recommend this to anyone who shares their life with a favorite pet. It's well written, fun, and inspiring. Great work!"

Join the Dogs Know Best Community

Join the Dogs Know Best Community

We're certain that dogs, and all types of pets for that matter, around the world are teaching their humans life lessons every day, more than we could include here. Do you have a life lesson that you've learned from your own dog, cat, bird, bunny, horse, or other favorite pet? We want to hear about it!

Go to http://petlifelessons.com to share your lesson, and to see expanded stories from Bimmer and Bertram. Tell us your story. Don't forget to include where you're from and a picture so we can see who the teacher is! You can also email your lesson to share@petlifelessons.com.

In the meantime, join our Facebook community at http://facebook.com/groups/dogsknowbest to catch up on the latest from Bimmer and Bertram and also to learn new lessons that others have shared.

We can't wait to hear from you!

To Lindsay,
Keep your nose pointed
the wind!

Bimmer & Berham

To my favorite co-authors,
your paw prints cover my heart.

To my husband, Tom, and to my family,
thank you for believing in me.

And to all the dog lovers out there,
this is for you!

Contents

Introduction

"The dog lives for the day, the hour, even the moment"
~ Robert Falcon Scott

"I so often found myself smiling, laughing, or tearing up as I wrote this book because of the incredible lessons I have learned from my two goofballs. Having a companion – much less two – like the ones that inspired me and taught me the lessons included here has absolutely made my life richer. To everyone who reads this book, I wish the same."
~ Angie Salisbury

Thursday, April 18, 2003 - As I slowed down to look for the right house number, I was excited and nervous at the same time. My stomach was doing cartwheels. It was my birthday, and I was about to meet my new puppies – I was bringing home two! I didn't really know what I was in for; I just knew that whatever it was, I was ready.

I parked on the street and walked up to the house. It was a tiny bungalow with a fenced in back yard – the kind of fence that envelops the driveway. As I approached the side, this little brown and white guy comes prancing out from the back yard and lets out a couple of his best ferocious "big dog" barks at me. Such a strong voice for a little guy. That brought the rest of the litter (and the two parents) over to see what was happening. Lots of barking and yipping, lots of excited bounding around – and not just from me!

The homeowner came to let me in, and instantly I was surrounded by six of the cutest German Shorthaired puppies I had ever seen; four others had already gone to their new forever homes. As I let myself be engulfed by the chaos that only a pack of energetic puppies can bring, I knew I was in trouble!

Once everyone settled down a little, we sat down at the picnic table to talk about the pups. Suddenly I looked to my side, and there's a brown little female with white feet who had her head in my purse, rooting through it showing early signs of being a pickpocket. So bold at such a young age. That did it; I knew she was coming home with me! We named her Bertram. My other choice? The first one I saw – the Head of Security – the brown and white guy who first barked at me. We named him Bimmer.

I was in love.

On the ride home, I'm not sure who was more nervous – the puppies or me. Once we got home from my white-knuckled drive – I had precious cargo on board – they immediately went to seek cover under the dining room table. They stayed there, mostly, for the better part of five hours, watching me with wide eyes. Sure, they'd come out to investigate me or a new toy or a treat, but always going back to their safe zone. I didn't mind. I spent most of that time on the floor with them, talking to them, playing with them, and waiting for them to come to me. I was oblivious to time passing or to chores going undone or to meals not made. I was mesmerized by these two little balls of brown and white fur that had now become part of our lives.

Typical of smart, strong-headed Pointers, it didn't take long before they settled in and took over the household. They quickly became comfortable and were following me around the house, watching, playing, and investigating. For two weeks all I did was ask, "Where are the puppies? What are the puppies doing? Where's the other one? What are they getting into?"

It was exhausting.

Each day with these two was an adventure filled with discovery and brought smiles and laughter. On the fourth day of being in our family, it was a beautiful Sunday spring morning, and we decided to take them to this wide open field on top of a hill in the Cuyahoga Valley National Park, just up the road from where we live. We thought it would be fun to run around, play, and explore. They were getting the hang of car rides already, and when we parked and let them out, they headed off to explore. As we started to go into the field, which was heavy with dew, our girl, Bertram, slowed down and started high-stepping through the grass, eventually stopping. She lifted up her front paws – first the right one, then the left – and looked back at us with an expression that seemed to say, "My feet are wet, and I'm not happy about it." She stood in place, licking the dew from her paws, until finally she gave in and went to chase her brother. Soon the pesky dew was a fleeting annoyance.

Fast-forward 12 years later, and these two still make

me laugh or smile every day. My heart warms when I see them together, when they "sing" to me, or give me a bump to let me know that it's dinnertime. They are my entertainment and my constant companions. They have taught me so much, and by sharing these lessons with you, I hope they can teach you a thing or two. At the very least, bring a smile to your face and some joy into your heart.

But I'll let them take over from here.

Meet the Pointers

"Since the German Shorthaired Pointer was developed to be a dog suited to family life as well as a versatile hunter, the correct temperament is that of an intelligent, bold, boisterous, eccentric, and characteristically affectionate dog that is cooperative and easily trained. Shyness, fearfulness, over submissiveness, aloofness, lack of biddability, or aggression (especially toward humans) are all incorrect traits. The GSP is usually good with children, although care should be taken because the breed can be boisterous especially when young. These dogs love interaction with humans and are suitable pets for active families who will give them an outlet for their considerable energy; they must be avidly run multiple times a week.

Most German Shorthaired Pointers make excellent watchdogs. The breed generally gets along well with other dogs, though females appear to be much more dominant during interbreed interaction. A strong hunting instinct is correct for the breed, which is not always good for other small pets such as cats or rabbits. With training, however, the family dog should be able to discern what is prey and what is not, and they can live quite amicably with other family pets."[1]

---

[1] Wikipedia.org

Bertram (left) and Bimmer (right), ready to go for a car ride.

Our names are Bimmer and Bertram. We're brother and sister German Shorthaired Pointers, and we love our human Mom and Dad. They brought us to our new home when we were just four months old; we're 12 now, so that's a long time ago. At first we didn't know what was happening when our soon-to-be Mom came to get us. I (Bimmer) barked at her, even then taking the lead on Safety & Security. Bertram rifled through her purse when she set it down on the bench, making sure she checked out, but really just looking for something good to take (she's still a pickpocket today). But new Mom just smiled at us, told us we were adorable, and asked if she could take us home.

It was love at first sight.

That was long ago, and since that first, scary car ride home, we've come to rule the house. It didn't take us long. No one can resist big, brown puppy dog eyes;

it's a scientific fact.

We've seen a lot, listened a lot, taught a lot, and learned a lot. We thought it was about time to share our philosophy and lessons on life with all of you humans so that you could have the same incredible life we do. Think of it as our legacy. Over the years we've continually proven that we're right – we hear one phrase over and over… "Never doubt the Pointers." It's true.

You guys often overlook the simple things. Life doesn't always have to be complicated. In fact, when things get stressful (like during a thunderstorm), that's when you have to get back to basics. Simple, little things can be a lot of fun or make you really happy. Case in point, when's the last time you played with an empty toilet paper roll?

While we have some valuable lessons to share, we had to call in help. We don't do too well on a keyboard, and Mom doesn't like it when we try to use her laptop; we've both tried and it didn't work out too well. So we're letting her do the typing. But again, we have big brown eyes that she can't resist, so she doesn't mind.

We've come up with a bunch of simple life lessons to help you live a life that is as happy as ours – we could have gone on and on, but Mom made us stop after a while. She said it was so anyone reading these tips would have a chance to start to incorporate them into their lives right away, but we secretly think she was getting tired of typing.

All together, these lessons make up how we live and explain why we're so happy, so fortunate. More importantly, we think they are good lessons for you guys to learn and mix into your daily life.

Here they are – our life lessons as we see them. After we tell you the lesson, we've included a brief "human translation" just in case you don't get it, so you know what to do with each one.

Don't just read them one time. Come back to these lessons whenever you need a refresher or whenever you feel like the world is getting too heavy for your shoulders.

After we've shared our lessons, we'll tell you how you can share any that your dogs (or other pets) have taught you! We know there are a lot of gifted canine teachers out there.

Accepting Yourself & Others

Your powdered sugar nose
is just perfect.

We were really adorable when we were puppies (as all puppies are), and as we've grown up, we've just gotten better and better. We have the wisdom that time brings in our eyes and have earned our powdered sugar noses. We're confident in who we are and don't let the fact that we're getting a day older dim that conviction. We still have a lot of room in our hearts for love. Plus, Mom tells us every day that we're beautiful and handsome inside and out, no matter what.

The Dog to Human Translation: Just because you have a little gray in your hair or a wrinkle by your eyes doesn't mean you're any less beautiful. Those things are just your surface and don't define who you are or showcase your true beauty. Your beauty shines from within – from your spirit, from your personality, from your soul. Age brings wisdom and confidence and that's one of the most beautiful things you can have. If there is something that you consider to be a flaw, take a good hard look in the mirror and recognize how those "flaws" combine to form your unique beauty. Embrace your "flaws" because you know what? They're not flaws. They're stepping stones on a beautiful path to accepting who you are as a complete person.

It's OK to use a ramp to get into the car.

There are some things that we just can't do, either because we're too short, don't have opposable thumbs, or can't wear the right kind of hat. But that's ok, because we know we can count on our Mom and Dad to help us out whenever we need it. As we're getting older, we need an extra helping hand for some things. After Bimmer had his knee surgeries (two torn ACLs, surgeries five months apart when he was just five years old), we started using a ramp to get in and out of the car. But now that we're 12 years old, we can't make that big jump so easily anymore, so the ramp is a big help for us. Bimmer's also having a little trouble getting up on the bed, so Mom or Dad will give him a boost to get up there at night. It's now known as "1-2-3 time." Once he gets upstairs, he'll stand by the bed. Mom will ask, "Are you ready? Let's do this in 1-2-3. OK? One!" That's when he gets a kiss on the top of his head. "Two!" She wraps her arms tight around him. "Three!" And up he goes. So now it's at the point where, in the evening, when he hears "1-2-3," he knows it's time to head up to bed.

> **The Dog to Human Translation:** When you're younger, it's natural to think you can do everything yourself – you feel invincible! But as you get older, you realize that there are times when you need help from someone else.

And that's ok. It may be hard initially to even ask for help or to accept help, but once you admit to yourself that you do need that helping hand, it's freeing. It takes the pressure off of you – a pressure that's been put there by many, many years of trying to do things on your own and be independent. Asking for help does not mean you're compromising your independence. Actually it's the opposite – it's being strong enough to acknowledge that you can't do it all by yourself, and enlisting someone else to be your partner for that moment or that activity shows strength. Many people love to help; helping others provides a feeling of worth. You never know – asking someone to reach for something on the top shelf, proofread your resume, pick up a prescription, shovel snow, or open the dog treat bag may provide someone with that much-needed feeling of usefulness just when they needed it most.

Take a break on your walk when you need one.

When we were pups we could keep going and going – whether chasing a ball at the dog park or trotting along on a five-mile walk. But as we get older, we know when it's time to stop and take a break. Lately, Bimmer's gotten especially good at this on our walks. When he gets tired and needs to stop for a rest, he'll slow down and stop. That lets Mom know that he needs a break, so she will call me back and we'll hang out until he's ready to go again. If it's a hot day, we'll stop in the shade under a tree, and while he rests, it gives me a chance to really investigate and sniff around, so I don't mind at all. When he's ready, he looks at Mom and gives her the high sign, and we're off again.

The Dog to Human Translation: When you're young, it seems like you can go forever. But as you get older, just like us, you'll need to take a break when you're tired or have to catch your breath. And that's ok. Listen to your body signals when they tell you to stop and recharge, especially when it's really hot and you're doing something strenuous. Don't push yourself just to prove to someone else that you don't need a break. It's ok; it's nothing to feel bad about. This lesson includes taking mental breaks too, because you humans are always "going to work."

When your mind gets too cluttered or overwhelmed, stop and take a break until you're ready to go again. It does a body – and mind – good.

Scars make you look tough at the dog park.

We know we're beautiful, but admittedly, we do have our imperfections. We have more gray in our noses than brown. Both of us are quite lumpy – we have what our doctor calls fatty tumors. Mom and Dad have them tested to make sure we're ok, but the lumps continue to grow. Bimmer has a few that are especially big, and they have caused him to slow down a bit. He gets thrown off balance easier. Mine are not so bad, but I have my fair share, too. We also have our fair share of scars. I've had a couple of cancer tumors removed, and Bimmer has had two very big surgeries to repair torn ligaments in his knees and still others to have fatty tumors removed. Despite all that, Mom and Dad think we're perfect, the most beautiful and handsome of dogs, and don't love us any less because we have some scars and bumps. In fact, the scars just make us look tough to the other dogs at the park.

The Dog to Human Translation: Everyone has scars, lumps, and bumps. Imperfections, gray hairs, wrinkles, maybe a hitch in your step, or some aches and pains – visible or invisible. But no matter what, you're perfect as you, just how you are because you're you. Those imperfections make you unique. Despite what you may think are imperfections, you're loved by people who don't even see them.

You're valued, honored, and held close in someone's heart. Some days you may forget that, and if you do have one of those days, you'll do well to take a few quiet moments and run through your list of those who are most important in your life and remind yourself of those very facts. Each one of these things adds up to form the unique being that is only you.

Persistence Leads to Happiness

Just because something's up on a counter doesn't mean it's out of reach.

We have a gift – all dogs do. We are very adept at figuring out how to get things that people think are out of reach. Leaving good smelling food out on the counter? Hardly a challenge; that's like an open door for us. We will figure out a way to get that food, no matter what we have to do. We tried this a lot more when we were younger, but we eventually had to tone down our thievery because it would make Mom and Dad angry, and we don't much like when that happens. But Bertram did manage to sneak a whole stick of butter when she was little, and she and I shared a cold, delicious Frappuccino from Starbucks when we were wee ones (come on, it was left in a car cup holder!).

> *The Dog to Human Translation:* When there's something that you really want in life, go after it. Find a way to get it. Don't let your own hesitations or doubts stop you or hold you back. Don't listen to the worries or fears going through your mind. You have the power to tell them all to be quiet and go someplace else while you go after what you want. Just because something appears to be out of reach, doesn't mean it actually is. You control your life. You can accomplish whatever you set your mind to.

The key is to use all your resources and to be persistent. Use your mind, your creativity, your energy, your strength, your voice. Tell others what you want and put your message out to the universe. Don't let anything stand in your way. If there is a hydrant or baby gate in your way, figure out how to get past it. Sometimes it may mean a shift in direction completely, but as long as you know the ultimate destination, you'll find a way to get there. Don't let failures get you down or make you give up. Just dust off and go at it again. And again. And again. Use your resources and your ingenuity and you'll be amazed at what you can take off the counter.

If you want to get someone's attention, bump them with your nose.

We're *masters* at this one. We have figured out how to get exactly what we want, when we want it, and most of the time we're successful. We're very persistent and don't give up easily. In addition to our big eyes, we have big voices to sing with and noses to nudge with. We are not afraid to tell Mom when we want a treat, when we're hungry, which direction we want to travel on a walk, when we're tired, when we need to cuddle, or when we want to be left alone (which, let's face it, doesn't happen often). Use what you have – your big dog voice or give your human a bump (a nose bump in their butt gets their attention every time!). Don't stop until you have their full attention. If they walk away, block their path by stepping in front of them. We've both been known to stop right in front of Mom during a walk when we wanted to turn around or go a different direction than she was heading. When it's time to eat and Mom is working, we'll take turns to tell her it's time. First we go for prolonged eye contact. Then we start to talk to her, increasingly getting louder and more and more forceful. Bertram is especially good at pawing at her when she pretends not to hear us; it works every time.

> **The Dog to Human Translation:** *Use your voice. Use what resources you have in front of you. If you don't have something, figure out how to get it.*

Be polite and don't be rude, but don't just sink into the background. You have a voice; you have an opinion and can give valuable input. So when you need to get someone's attention, say something.

Never pass up a chance
to photo bomb.

Dogs are masters at the photo bomb. We (collectively) don't like being left out of a good family photo or selfie. If someone insists that we can't be in the picture, we'll go behind everyone and hang out in the background. Why? Because we want to be included and be a part of the pack. We are family members, and since we can't actually take the photo (that thumb-thing again), we'll be in it. And let's face it, every picture is going to be better with a big dog nose in it!

The Dog to Human Translation: Capture fun times with friends and family with a photograph; don't miss the opportunity to create a new memory. Don't forget about the quiet times. Memorialize the every day. So go ahead, take that group selfie so you can be a part of the commemoration rather than hiding behind the lens. And if you can't be directly in the photo, practice your best photo bomb!

Building Relationships

"Let the dove fly away so you can chase it again tomorrow."

Even though we're 12 years old, we still have to listen to our Mom because she will always make sure we're safe and happy. She won't let us do anything that will get us in trouble or may get us hurt. Occasionally we're not happy about it, like when we're trying to eat something extra special that we found on our walk. Or if we're really close to catching that mourning dove we've been stalking. But she will tell us that we have to let the dove fly away so we can chase it again tomorrow, or we'll have a tummy ache if we eat that really yummy treasure we found, so we reluctantly have to listen and let the dove fly away or leave our treasure behind (but trust us, we'll remember exactly where it is and try again on our next walk).

The Dog to Human Translation: Like it or not, no matter how old you are, sometimes you have to listen to your Mom or Dad or mentor or trusted friend because they will know what will keep you safe or happy. It's true, so don't try and fight this fact. Even if you think you're worldly, experienced, smart, or wise, you can always count on that one person in your life – likely when you least expect it. They have this inherent ability to see your life and your path and offer advice that will point you in the right direction.

You may not realize it while they're telling you, but maybe an hour later, a day later, or even after a year, you'll realize that they really did know what's best for you. But in order for this to happen it means being open and receptive to what someone else is saying. Try to resist the urge to think you know it all. No one knows it all. We can learn from the life experience that others have, and being open to that can make you rich beyond your imagination.

After going to the vet you'll get to have a treat.

At least once a year, our Mom and Dad make us go to the doctor, and we are not happy about it. Sure we enjoy the car ride getting there and trot right into the building, but we're not happy about being there once we find out we have to go inside(even though everyone there is so friendly and we can usually visit with other dogs while we wait our turn – sometimes we even get to check out a cat, although we can't figure out why they're always in a box looking at us through a door.). When our doctor is done looking at us, we get to have a treat or two and are told how good we are. We don't like getting baths, either. We're told we have to get a bath so we stay soft and shiny… and don't stink! We'll try and worm our way out of the tub, but haven't been successful yet. When we're done, we get ruffled by a big fluffy towel, which we love! When it's bath time but it's cold outside, Mom helps us get warm and dry with the blow dryer, which I consider to be an extra bonus (although Bertram doesn't like the loud noise, so much). We don't like to do these things, but we'll do them because Mom said it's something we have to do for some good reason, and we trust her.

> *The Dog to Human Translation:* We all have to do things we don't necessarily want to do, but we have to do them, especially if someone we trust asks.

It's either for our own good (going to the dentist), will help someone else (doing some extra housework for an aging parent or taking a child for their flu shot),or it's just the right thing to do (the dreaded office party). No matter what, try to remember that when it's over, you can treat yourself to something special – a favorite beverage, a massage, a favored sweet treat, or a long walk in the park with your favorite four-legged friend. Turn your attitude and make the best of a challenging situation. But don't pass on doing things you have to do because you're too stubborn. Take a deep breath, face it head on, and relish your reward.

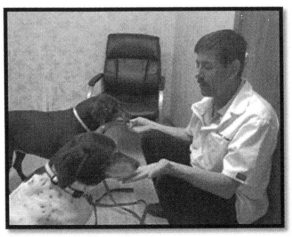

Getting checked out by our favorite vet, Dr. Douglas Paroff

Love doesn't ask for anything in return.

We love our Mom and Dad no matter what. We will do anything for them. We love each other too. We are protective and will watch over each other, no matter against other animals, dogs, or people. It's just what we do. We don't ask for anything in return. The fact that we do get something – love, scratches, walks, treats, toys, car rides – that's just a bonus. We'd be there for our family, no matter what.

> **The Dog to Human Translation:** Don't put conditions on your love and friendship. If you offer it to someone, it is a gift that you are giving freely. Don't expect something in return. If you get something back – love, friendship, companionship, guidance – that's just a bonus. Be there for the other person, no matter what.

Step in when the giant dog won't stop playing.

We look out for each other, and for those in our family. We're protectors and take that job very seriously. When we go to the dog park and another dog isn't being too friendly with one of us – or *overly* friendly – the other one will step in and let them know. One time when we were at the dog park, a big Great Dane was chasing me. I had to run very fast to keep ahead of him because he had much longer legs than me. It was fun at first, but after a while I got tired because he wouldn't leave me alone. Bimmer was watching and when he saw that I was losing ground, he came running over and got between me and the giant dog so I could get away. When we're out and someone approaches our Mom or Dad, we check them out to make sure he or she is safe. If someone comes to the door of our house, we'll make it known, in no uncertain terms, that they have to get past us before they are allowed inside.

The Dog to Human Translation: Keep an eye out for each other. It doesn't have to be with just family members, but your friends, acquaintances, and neighbors... even complete strangers. Every once in a while, ask if they're ok. Ask if they need help. Offer a smile or a willing ear to listen. Most importantly, be kind to each other. You have to be protectors of those who come into your lives, and it is a role you should take very seriously, just like we do.

There's enough love to go around.

We had a lot of brothers and sisters when we were little – there were eight other Pointer puppies in our family… 10 of us plus our parents! So, we had to learn how to share – our food, our toys, our bed. But that was a good experience because now Bimmer and I are very good about sharing everything. We'll share our food, our chew bones, toys, and even our affection. We have never fought over something that the other one had. In fact, we've very good about waiting our turn to get food or water. We'll play tug of war with a toy, but don't get mad when the other one ends up with it. We'll just go chase and try and get it back. I do get a little jealous if Mom is giving Bimmer more attention than she is giving me, so I'll try and worm my way in to the mix – she's got enough love for both of us, but I want my fair share!

The Dog to Human Translation: You know this one already, but we'll say it one more time. Sharing is good. Share your heart, share your ideas, share your wisdom, share your love, share your knowledge, share your time. Don't always try to be putting a price on those things. Share what you have and others don't. If you are able, share your food and your wealth. Giving to others will make you a very rich person.

Sometimes it's important
not to walk away.

We know there are times when Mom just needs us to listen to her. She is not expecting a response from us, but we know it's important that we look at her while she is talking to us and not walk away to look out the window or leave the room. We don't always know what she's talking about, but we can tell that it matters to her. Sometimes she seems upset; other times she's excited or concerned. No matter, we're happy to be there while she talks it out.

> **The Dog to Human Translation:** Being a good friend to someone means that you're willing and able to listen to them. Not just hear them, but to actually listen to what they are saying... and not saying. There will be times when that is the most important gift you can give to them. Listen without judgment and without criticism. You may not even need to respond or say anything, but just be there.

Speak up when you need a blanket.

We're a vocal pair. We both are quite chatty and will use our voices to get what we want. We have a big vocabulary and use it to our advantage. We have ways to explain when we're hungry, when we want to play, when we're content, when we're nervous, or when we need to be covered by a blanket and can't quite get it on our own (thumbs). We will say something when we want to go for a walk or be otherwise entertained. On top of that, we'll bump and nudge as necessary to get attention. When there are times when we want to be left alone, we have ways to convey that message too. Bertram will actually leave the room and go to sleep in a quiet, dark spot when she's extra sleepy. I don't like to be alone as much, so the most I'll do is go to another room, but rarely out of earshot, just in case I am needed.

The Dog to Human Translation: You can't read minds, no matter how well you think you know someone – or how well someone knows you. So it's important if you want something to say so. Tell someone what you want and why. Don't be demanding or mean, and certainly don't expect that you'll get what you want every time. But if you are able to articulate your needs, wants, and desires with those around you, the chances of achieving your goals will increase dramatically.

Speak from your heart and be truthful. Don't cloud a request in lies, deception, or secrecy. Don't assume someone will be able to "figure it out" by themselves. They have their own things going on in their minds. The same is true if you want to be left alone, physically or mentally. If you need some space and time to be alone, processing your thoughts or clearing your head, say so. It's better to get it out there than to hold on to false expectations or create resentment.

We're not happy if
our tail is down.

When we're not happy or are not feeling too well for some reason, we find a way to let our Mom or Dad know. We tell them with our eyes, with our body language, how we hold our ears and our tails. Depending on what is wrong, we may ask to go outside or lay down next to them just to be close. Every once in a while it's even meant a trip to see the doctor. It's no different than when we're happy. If we don't let them know something is wrong, they won't be able to help us. Now if the tables are turned and we see that something is wrong with one of our humans, we become very concerned. We will watch them closely, follow them, or sit quietly at their side. We don't need an explanation; our job is to give them back the same love and support that they give to us every day.

The Dog to Human Translation: *From time to time, you may want to just keep something to yourself – maybe you're sad, angry, or not feeling too well. That's ok if you just need a little breathing room or space to be by yourself and sort something out in your own mind. But if it starts to feel overwhelming or you can't seem to shake the feeling, go to someone you trust and ask for help. Tell them what the problem is and how they may be able to help you.*

If it's something that is too much for them to handle, they can be the one to help find the right person or professional. There's no reason to try and go it alone. We're all social creatures, and we build communities to help and support each other. We have an instinct to help, so don't be afraid to tap into the abundance that is the generosity and caring of others. This works in reverse, also. If you see someone who needs help, is sad, angry, or feeling lonely, reach out and extend your help. Offer to find additional help. Don't be content to sit by and think, "Oh, they'll snap out of it." That snap may not come or may take entirely too long to happen. Be there for each other, and don't expect anything in return.

If you don't want someone to leave, sit on their feet.

We do this one a lot. When we want to make sure our Mom or Dad stays put, we'll sit on or lay across their feet. This way they can't go anywhere; eventually they get the hint and just stay put. Why would we do this? It happens if we've had a lot to do that day between walks, car rides to the store, maybe even a visitor to the house, and now want to just take a nap. Sometimes it's because we're comfortable, frankly, and don't feel like moving and want them to stay and be our pillow.

> ***The Dog to Human Translation:*** *You can sit on someone's feet if you want to and don't mind the funny looks, but you may have more luck if you actually tell someone you don't want them to leave. Ask them to stay with you; share the reasons why you need their company and companionship at that moment. Chances are, they'll stay if they can, just as if you sat on their feet. If they can't stay, ask when they can come back to be with you.*

It's ok to be frightened during a storm.

Although we're tough dogs, we're not overly brave. There are some things that we just don't like – loud rain or thunderstorms, the sound of the smoke alarm, or when Dad's using the nail gun to fix something. Those noises make us scared and we won't relax until long after they have stopped. When there's a loud noise we don't like, we will look for Mom or Dad because we know they'll help keep us safe. They will try to distract us or tell us everything is going to be ok. Sometimes they'll even leave the house with us until the noise has stopped; for example, Mom will take us out for a walk while Dad finishes his repair. Or when one of the smoke alarms in the house malfunctioned one night, Mom took us out for a car ride while Dad stayed back at home while the fire chief made sure everything was safe. That doesn't mean we're still not scared, but we trust that they will not let anything happen to us.

The Dog to Human Translation: *When something in life scares you, seek out the company of someone you trust, someone you know will make you feel safe: a friend, a family member, a coworker, a neighbor, or a counselor. Life can bring all kinds of scary noises and situations, but the wonderful thing about that is you don't have to go through them alone.*

There will be someone to offer a hug and some kind words, advice or guidance, and protection. You need to find that person and tell them what's happening and how they can help you. They may not know automatically so it's up to you to tell them. But once they know, they will be there with you to get you past that scary situation. We can't all be brave all the time, and there are things that may seem scary to one person and not to another. In times like this, it's about helping each other out and being there to support one another. Being scared doesn't mean you're weak. In fact, it's the opposite – it shows your strength of character to be open to reach out to another person for comfort.

Be there when things get tough for others.

Pointers are very intuitive. We know when our Mom is having a bad day or if she's upset. That's when we jump into action and stick close, leaning in for a snuggle or offering to be scratched behind the ear or under our chin. We look at her with our big brown eyes, reminding her that we love her and we'll stick by her no matter what. It always works because we'll be rewarded with a smile, gentle words whispered in our ears, or a cuddle.

The Dog to Human Translation: Be there for others – friends, loved ones, a stranger. Be available. This means being willing to open up and give part of yourself to someone else. It's looking outside yourself and shifting your focus to another person. That may be in the form of a listening ear or advice from your heart. Pay attention to what's going on around you. If you see someone is having a bad day or is upset, be there for them to listen, to comfort. If someone is struggling to do something, step in with an offer to help. If they can't reach something in a store, grab it for them. If a package is too heavy, offer to carry it. If there is a tear, offer a shoulder. Being there for others may mean putting your own agenda or schedule aside temporarily and making room for someone else.

It may mean sitting with them quietly, listening, offering a kind smile or a shoulder to lean on. Don't ask for anything in return, but don't worry, when it comes time for you to need a shoulder(and it will happen because it happens to all of us) someone will be there for you – a friend, family member, or stranger. We remember once when Mom was taking us to doggie daycare one morning and she was not having a good morning at all. She was running late, she spilled her coffee, she was dreading the meeting she had to go to, and on top of everything else, traffic was slow. We were waiting at a traffic light, and we pulled up next to the school bus we had been following for the last several miles. We knew because Mom kept talking about the "damn school bus." Mom looked over (and it wasn't a very happy look!) and in the window of the bus was a little girl, maybe seven or eight years old, with a smile that went from ear to ear. She gave Mom a big wave. Mom smiled and gave a big wave back. The little girl even smiled at us – she was a cutie! But after that, Mom was calmer, she told us how much that little girl's kind gesture meant to her, so we know it made her feel good. She was ready to pass that goodness on to someone in her day. It's a beautiful cycle.

Wag your tail when you're happy to see someone.

When we're happy to see someone, we wiggle our short little tails as fast as we can to let them know. We'll go in for the kiss. This tells them that we've missed them, and we're happy to see them; we're ready to be petted or played with and need their attention.

The Dog to Human Translation: When you're happy to see someone, "wag your tail" and let them know – tell them, give them a hug or a kiss, or shake their hand. Share a big smile. Don't be embarrassed or feel like you have to hold back. Don't worry about what others around you may say; it's about letting the other person know they are important to you, and that's what matters.

Dogs are intuitive; we've got you covered

Dogs are very intuitive when it comes to figuring out humans. We instinctively know when you're feeling happy, sad, angry, silly, excited, nervous, anxious, hurt, or frightened. We just know. In fact, scientists have proven that we're *wired* to pick up on your mood changes – or mood swings, in some cases. We have learned how to read your facial expressions, listen to the tone of your voice, and watch your movements. We have been studying you for years, so we know what's happening. When you're happy, we're happy with you. When you're sad, we'll snuggle in and offer a furry head in comfort on your lap. When you're angry, we'll look you in the eye and listen if you need to talk it out, or we'll stay out of your way if you need a little space (but not too far out of sight so we're ready to jump back in when you're ready). We don't judge you for your emotions, and we won't criticize you. We won't think any less of you when you cry, but we might give you a friendly "woof" if you're being too silly! So don't worry, we've got you covered.

---

*The Dog to Human Translation: Pay attention to those around you – your friends, family, co-workers – and react how they need you to react. Watch their facial expressions and body movements. Listen to their vocal tone and inflections. Listen to what they are **not** saying.*

The better you know someone, the better you'll be able to pick up on subtle changes. Don't let those changes go unnoticed. When they're happy, be happy with them. Sad? Offer a gentle shoulder to lean on. Angry? Listen to their frustration and offer support and, if asked, advice. Anxious? Be a calming presence. Don't judge, don't criticize. Don't minimize the feelings. Just be with them in their journey, and they'll be there for you.

"Sorry I chewed the emergency brake handle."

Occasionally we will do something that makes our Mom or Dad angry or upset. We emphasize *occasionally* because we're pretty much perfect, but things do happen. (Mom doesn't like when Bertram outsmarts the barrier system in the car and ends up in the front seat, defiantly sitting next to the chewed up emergency brake handle. That's happened three times.) On the rare occasions when we do get in trouble, we let them know we're sorry. After a few minutes, we'll go up to them with big eyes, asking if everything is ok between us again. If they're not ready, we'll try again after another few minutes. This time, in addition to the eyes, we'll close in tight for a scratch. If we have to pull out the big guns, we'll nuzzle into them and put our head on their lap. That usually does the trick and before we know it, we're getting a big kiss on our head (maybe even a treat).

The Dog to Human Translation: If you do something to upset someone else and you're aware of it, say you're sorry. Offer the apology and explain why what you did or said was wrong. Don't just give a flip, "Sorry." Let the person know that you're aware of your actions. We know it's not easy to admit when you've done something wrong, but it's the right thing to do.

It shows real strength of character and awareness of yourself and the impact your words or actions have on other people. If someone needs a little time before they're ready to accept your apology, that's ok. Give them the space, but don't give up trying. Show them that they are important enough to you to keep trying.

Bertram makes friends with a bee.

Not only are we great with you people, but our friends come in all shapes and sizes. In fact, Bertram has a special fondness for the big bees that come to visit us every summer (sometimes she gets a little too enthusiastic and bites one, but she's really just trying to play). They are big as a blimp and hover in one place for a long time and then shoot away, all the while making this loud buzzing sound. She thinks it's great fun to chase them and will do it for hours in summer. We've even named the bee "Carl," so when she hears that Carl is outside, she goes off to find him. We like birds, bunnies, and chipmunks. Frogs and turtles are a little confusing, and snakes make us jump. We love seeing cows and horses and the occasional deer. Wild turkeys are exciting because they are very fast, like us. We love our neighbor dog, and he's much smaller than us. We've heard about other dogs being friends with really big animals and really small critters. What matters to us is each animal or person has some quality about them that we really like, no matter what they look like.

The Dog to Human Translation: Don't judge people just because they look or act differently from you. It's about finding that one thing – that connection; it's not about whether they look or act or think just like you, because where's the fun in that?

Accept that we all are unique and have our own beautiful features and our own set of life experiences. We all have something that makes us rare – a one of a kind. When you do meet someone new, offer a handshake, a "Hello," or a smile. Don't rush to make judgments about people just because of how they look, what they're wearing, or what they're doing. Take a moment to get to know them and discover what you have in common and share what makes you unique. You may just be surprised to find that you are more alike than you think!

Bertram eye-to-eye with her bee friend, Carl.

Look others in the eye.

Dogs are one of the few animals that will seek out eye contact with humans. We look at you to learn information, to figure out what's going on with you, and to learn about our world around us. We are very observant and are great at reading you, and one of the ways we do that is by watching you and looking you in the eye. It helps us make sense of what's going on around us and make sure we get what we want. You could say we're very polite.

> ***The Dog to Human Translation:*** *Look others in the eye when you're interacting with them. Show the other person that you are interested in what they have to say and that you are paying attention to your interaction with them. Making eye contact helps you focus and be present in the moment, giving them your full attention. It tells them that they are important to you. It doesn't matter whether you're interacting with someone from work or the cashier at the grocery store. When you're talking and interacting with someone else, put your phone down, don't try to see who is over their shoulder, and look at the person you're dealing with to give them the respect they deserve.*

Teamwork gets the dove.

Since we were little, we've been tag-teaming. When we meet a new dog, we both go wide and approach (ok, stalk) from opposite sides. Sometimes the other dog is not too happy about that because they aren't sure which one of us to watch, but this way we keep an eye on them and make sure they don't escape! Last summer was a particularly good bird flushing and catching season for us (much to Mom's chagrin). We have it down to a science and work together really well as a team. Our system went like this: I would lock in on the bird. It was usually a mourning dove sitting under a pine tree (mourning doves are not real smart, but they make a nice loud cooing noise and are slow to get out of the way). That would get Bertram's attention, and she would move into stalking position, usually opposite of me. Then I would pounce, flushing the bird up, and Bertram would move in for the catch. It worked like a charm for about three weeks, but then Mom started to get a little upset with all of our victories and wouldn't let us do as much stalking for a while. One time we missed the catch, but as the dove got away, a hawk almost got it – it was very exciting as they flew back and forth over our heads! Mom wouldn't let us go under this certain group of pine trees for a while, until the doves decided to move to a different area. But it was our top-notch teamwork that got the job done.

The Dog to Human Translation: There will be times when you need to work as part of a team, whether it's with just one other person or a group. But there can be power in the many. When you are in a situation that requires teamwork, communicate with each other. Find out what your individual strengths are and learn how those can combine to achieve your outcome. Make sure you're all working towards the greater goal. It's ok to be a loner or to work individually, but there will be a time that calls for the input of someone else. And when that happens, know how you're going to approach the mourning dove – who is going to lock in, stalk, and pounce, and who is going to catch. Clarify your roles before you get started, but be ready to adjust as necessary.

Spend quiet time with the ones you love.

We love to be around our Mom and Dad all the time – Pointers didn't earn the nickname "Velcro dogs" for nothing – but especially when they are sitting down for a bit of quiet time reading, watching TV, or just relaxing. One of our favorite times is after we have our dinner, but Mom has not started making her dinner yet. She'll sit on the couch, and we'll hop up on either side of her, settle in, and take a nap with our heads on her lap. Or in the early mornings when Mom and Dad are awake but we're not ready to face the day, we come downstairs to be with them and cuddle in to finish our sleep. Or on a nice day we will go out on the front porch and just hang out with one of them, watching the cars and people in the neighborhood go by. In any of those examples we're not doing much, but we're together and that's what matters.

The Dog to Human Translation: *Spending time with those you care about doesn't always have to be flashy, full of excitement or adventure. The best memories can come from spending quiet time together. Maybe you're not even saying anything to each other; just being together is enough to make you happy. Make it a Point (pun intended) to be together and share the same space.*

Go for a walk, share a meal, enjoy a walk through the park or along the shoreline. You never know what you'll take away from that experience, be it a sense of peace, a feeling of being loved, a better understanding of each other, or a recognition of a strength in the other person you never knew they had.

Simple
Happiness

Is it a leaf or a critter?
Let's go find out!

Some of our favorite things are what you humans consider to be simple things – leaves that flutter in the wind, empty water bottles, empty toilet paper rolls, and even boxes. Sure, we like playing with our toys or chewing on a good bone every now and then, but when we can find a treasure on our own, it's something special. Another favorite thing? Going for a car ride. How could that not be exciting?!We love going for car rides, especially when we get to go through the country or the park on nice days (we don't like going into the big cities too much, all the excitement is in the country). The windows are down and we get to hear the birds, smell all the good smells, and see the animals. We get to go on an adventure, be with our favorite humans, and see new things. There are so many more things we could mention, but you get the idea.

The Dog to Human Translation: Every day, make sure you're noticing the small things around you. Listen to the sounds, look at the leaves on the trees, really see the colors. Take a deep breath on a clear fall day. Go outside during the first snowfall of the season. Look at the people you interact with at the office or in a store. Get off autopilot and start to experience every day.

Notice the simple things in your life and realize how important or special they can be. Something doesn't have to be fancy or expensive to be special. Don't take things for granted because those little things all add up to something really fantastic.

Notice something new and exciting in the routine of your life.

As part of our normal routine, twice a day, we go for a walk around our neighborhood. Mom likes to mix it up for us and take different routes (she often lets us decide when to turn or cross the street), but we're still staying in our neighborhood. For us, though, every walk is exciting. We get to go out and see and smell what's been happening since the last time we were there. We look for the birds, bunnies, chipmunks, and if we're lucky, a groundhog or a flock of geese or turkeys (or even a deer!). We sniff around to learn which of our dog friends have been out and about. We run through the long grasses because it tickles our bellies. We'll try and bring home an acorn or pinecone or some other fantastic treasure. We're excited every time we get to go out because we know we'll find something new.

The Dog to Human Translation: All people have routlnes, whether you go to work everyday or are home taking care of your kids (both 2-legged and 4-legged). Even if your daily schedule doesn't vary much, it's important to discover something new in each day. It goes back to that appreciation of the little things in life we told you about earlier. Each new day brings a new environment.

If you really do think things never change in your day, we challenge you to look very closely and pay attention tomorrow and find what is different. Make it a game and stretch your frame of reference to observe and recognize the world around you. Or even the world within yourself. Write down what you see in a "One New Thing" list. Soon enough, when you look back on your new discoveries, you'll very quickly realize that things are not the same every day.

Be silly for no reason.

We get goofy, sometimes for no reason at all and with no warning. It may start by poking Mom with our nose or diving into our toy pile. Then it's a free for all! Mom may look at us and say, "Where is this coming from?" and when she does, we'll give her a big bark in response. What other things do we do? Bimmer loves to roll down a hill in the grass or dig to the bottom of our toy pile, scattering them all around the room. I am a fan of unrolling the toilet paper from the bathroom. We love playing together, pouncing and play bowing and taking turns chasing each other around the house or yard. Snowballs are tons of fun, and we are always eager to "help" when it's time to shovel.

The Dog to Human Translation: There is so much in life that is serious – work, bills, the news, illness, and on and on. In order to keep your sanity and hold some lightness in your step, you have to let yourself get silly once In a while. What that means for you depends on how you define silly; it will be different for everyone. Maybe you go puddle-jumping right after a heavy rain. Maybe you draw funny faces and laugh at the best of the lot. Maybe you do your favorite dance with abandon. Have you played on a swing set lately?

Don't worry about whether someone might see you or what they might think because it really doesn't matter. Try not to think, "I'm too old to do that." Give yourself permission to get a little nutty and let the weight of the world roll down your back. You'll feel much lighter and better able to face the next challenge.

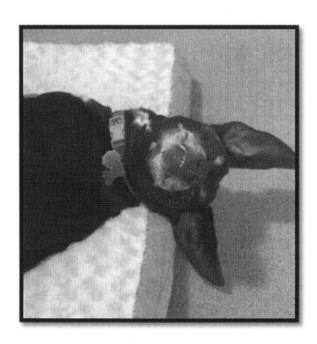

Comfort in a "go-to" toy.

We are lucky – we have a lot of fun toys to play with and always have a bone nearby if we want to chew on it. But of all our toys, there is always one or two that we like best of all, and those are the ones that we go back to again and again. These are the ones we'll look for, digging up our toy pile until we find it, ignoring the others, going from room to room, trying to figure out where we left it last time we played with it. For Bimmer it's a blue doggie; for me it's the red Angry Bird toy (it giggles when I bite it in the right spot). During quiet times, when we're not napping but we're also not playing or keeping watch, we'll look for our bone and chew it for a while. It's soothing and calming for us (not to mention it helps keep our teeth clean!).

The Dog to Human Translation: Find comfort in a favorite thing. You all have that "go-to" item – a favorite t-shirt, a stuffed bear, a special locket, or an old blanket. Maybe you like it so much because it is warm and cozy, evokes a certain memory, or reminds you of a special vacation. Mom has a special bear that means a lot to her – she's had it since she was a little girl and it's one toy that we're not allowed to play with, no matter how many times we ask (she keeps it up on a very high shelf, out of our reach). Embrace the fact that it is special to you.

> You don't need to explain it to anyone else; it doesn't matter whether they understand or not. What matters is the item is special to you and it's something you want to keep close to your heart.

If you find a treasure, share it with someone special.

When we're out for a walk or for playtime, we might get lucky and find a treasure – an empty water bottle, a paper cup, a good stick, or something even more interesting like a bird. When we do, we are sure to bring it home with us... all the way in to the house if we can, and share it with someone special. One time I found a bunny carcass and tried to give it to Mom. Bimmer even tried to convince her. She kept backing away from me so I had to really be persistent in my efforts to give it to her. In the end she traded it for an especially yummy treat so I did let her have it. I knew she wanted it. Share your treasures. Trust me, your humans will thank you.

The Dog to Human Translation: Something doesn't have to be fancy to be a treasure. When you're out on a walk or out for playtime and you find a pretty leaf, a flower, a colorful bug, or an acorn, pick it up or take a picture of it (leave the bug alone, don't bring it home) and share it with someone special. All those little treasures are what make up a rich life, so don't just walk past them. Share your enthusiasm for your little moments – it's sure to be contagious and might just bring a smile to someone's face.

Turn your nose into the wind and take a deep breath.

Windy days are our favorite! Except in the middle of winter when the wind makes it too cold on our walks (that's when we'll walk close behind Mom and use her as a shield). When the wind is blowing, we love to go outside, turn our noses into the breeze, and just inhale all the good smells! We can stand there for a long time taking it all in: the smell of the trees, the grass, the birds, the animals, other dogs, and general neighborhood smells (is someone grilling a steak?). You'd be surprised what you can find out when you do that. We love how the wind feels as we walk down to the trail. It makes our ears flap around and sometimes even blows a treasure across our path.

The Dog to Human Translation: Go outside on a windy day and turn your face into the breeze. Feel the air wash over you. Take a deep breath and inhale the world around you. Taking that moment to experience what nature brings you is a wonderful way to clear your mind and refresh your spirit. This works especially well when you're in the middle of a long day or challenging situation. It's a perfect way to recharge and is so simple, yet so powerful. Give it a try the next time you see the trees swaying in the wind... go out and be a part of it!

Discover a hobby.

Pointers are very smart dogs, so we need things to do to keep us busy and as an outlet for all of our smarts; otherwise we get into what Mom calls mischief. So over the years we've discovered some hobbies. We've been telling you about them already. A few favorites are chewing on a bone, playing with our toys, going for a hike in the woods, finding treasures hidden outside or throughout the house, watching what's going on in the neighborhood, or (Bertram's favorite) unrolling toilet paper. We have friends who do a bunch of different things like swimming, running agility courses, tracking, or actually going hunting. Having that favorite thing to do makes us happy, keeps our minds sharp, and is something we can either do by ourselves or together with our humans.

The Dog to Human Translation: Find something to do to keep your mind and spirit sharp. Discover what it is that you love doing and embrace it with abandon. If you don't know exactly what that is, try out a bunch of different things: a new sport, painting, building things, fixing things, making things, cooking, and on and on. Find your outlet and nurture your passion. It doesn't have to be meaningful or substantial to anyone else; it just has to be something you love doing. Then, when you need time by yourself or want to share your passion with a friend, you always have something to do.

Bury your nose in the snow.

We live in the north where it snows a lot. So when there's a lot of snow on the ground, there's nothing more fun than to go outside and bury your nose in the deep snow. It tickles your whiskers, and it's fun to tunnel through. Mostly, it's just a way to fully embrace the fun that a big snow brings.

The Dog to Human Translation: If you're so inclined, go ahead and bury your nose in the snow– we won't judge you! But what we're really suggesting here is that you embrace what life gives you and find true pleasure in the things that may not seem all that great on the surface. A lot of snow? Grab your sled or put on your boots and build a fort or a snow dog. Raining? Grab an umbrella and do your best "Singing in the Rain" impersonation. Big winds? When's the last time you flew a kite? It's become too common when there's extreme weather to stay inside and complain. But really, there's no reason to! Who cares if you get wet – you'll dry off. It's cold and snowy? Put on a hat and scarf and an extra layer or two and head out. Too hot? Take some layers off and find some water to cool off in – even if it's coming from the garden hose. Don't let excuses rob you of adventures.

Warm your belly in the sun.

We both love laying outside on a warm day, basking in the sunshine. We have our own small door in the big screen door to the deck that we use to let ourselves out. If it's closed, we'll ask Mom or Dad over and over again to go outside. We'll lie in the sun until we get too hot, then go back inside to cool off before wanting to go out again. It's a time for us to nap, smell the air around us, and listen to the birds and sounds of our neighborhood. In summer, I love stalking and snapping at those big wood-boring bees (you heard about the bees earlier, remember?), but Bimmer doesn't like them and when he sees or hears me do that, he runs back inside to find a different sun spot to lay in. It's almost like we are playing a game of chase, sometimes for an hour at a time. Unfortunately for the bee, at least a few times a year I actually catch one, but another one always shows up to continue the game. When it's cold outside, we'll find a sun spot inside so we can still get nice and warm while we nap.

> *The Dog to Human Translation: Being outside is a chance to recharge and get away from the mundane, draining things in your lives – work, the phone, chores, really any of the stresses of everyday human life. Make sure that you get outside every day and take a deep breath and let yourself relax. Do this even if it's really cold and snowy out.*

If you can't get to a park or the beach, find a quiet spot near you that you can call your own, and give yourself a little time in your day to recharge. Find your own "bee to chase" and warm your belly.

Practical Living

Never leave home without your ID.

We are not allowed to leave the house, even for a car ride, without wearing our nametags and licenses – Mom calls them our "driver's licenses." This way, in case anything happens, someone kind can help us get back home. We don't wear our collars to bed at night, but every morning when we "get dressed," we know we're starting another day filled with potential excitement.

The Dog to Human Translation: This one's really simple. Don't leave home without your ID or driver's license. In case something happens, someone kind can help you get back home. Here's an extra tip that a lot of people don't think about: put emergency contact information for your pets in your wallet or in your smartphone. Our Mom carries a card in her wallet and information in her phone letting people know about us in case we're not with her. It tells whom to call in case something happens to her, so that we're taken care of until her or Dad come back home.

Wear a life vest when swimming or a sweater when it's cold.

We don't do a lot of actual swimming, but our cousin in Florida is a real water dog. One thing we've learned from him is to never go swimming without your life vest on. His Mom makes him wear it just so nothing happens to him, whether he's in the ocean or a pool. This way he's safe but can still have a super good time playing in the water. Since we live in the north, we have to wear our sweaters when we go out in the winter and it's very cold. We don't have really thick fur coats of our own (come on, German *Shorthaired* Pointers),and we get pretty cold, so Mom got us these nice thick sweaters that we can wear to stay warm and still enjoy our walks. We have to say, they look pretty stylish, too.

The Dog to Human Translation: Always take necessary precautions to keep yourself safe. Wear a sweater when it's cold. If there is protective gear or equipment for what you're doing, make sure you use it. Don't take any chances, especially if there is a high degree of risk; it's just not worth it. You can still have fun, and you may even enjoy it more knowing you're ready for what may come your way. And heck, why be cold when you don't have to be?

Don't wear shoes that are uncomfortable.

We hate wearing boots. When we were younger Mom would try and make us wear them in winter when it was snowy or icy out. We did not want any part of the boots and would wiggle and squirm and pull our paws away because they felt funny. Anything to not have them put on our feet. When she did manage to get one on, we'd either stand still and not move or try and shake them off by lifting our feet up really high. Eventually we won and she stopped trying to put them on. Now when it's too cold or too icy (especially as we're getting older), we get to stay inside and keep our paws safe.

The Dog to Human Translation: If you have a pair of shoes that are uncomfortable, don't wear them. If, when you put them on, you try and shake them off or just stand there because they hurt when you walk in them, don't wear them. In fact, take a nice stroll around the store before you buy them. If they come to your house in a fun box (like the kind we always want to play with) delivered by a man in a brown outfit (who we always bark at until he gives us a treat), then wear them around the house for a while. Go up and down the stairs, do laundry in them, run up and down the hallway. Just don't go outside with them 'cause then you're stuck with them.

Try them on with your favorite outfit and make sure they get four paws up! Why is this important? Because wearing uncomfortable shoes will eventually make you grumpy and take your attention away from being able to focus on what's important in your life. You'll be thinking about how much your feet hurt, rather than saying hello to someone you pass, focusing on doing your best work, or noticing a winning smile.

Learn your neighborhood.

When we were little pups, Mom and Dad would take us out for long walks around our neighborhood. For us it was great fun exploring, but we didn't realize we were being taught a really valuable lesson – where we live and what's around our neighborhood. We learned what streets we can't cross and how to navigate the routes to get back home. This came in very handy one day when we had a puppy sitter who didn't know our neighborhood. Mom told her that we could go for a walk and to not worry, we would help find the way home. She took us for a long walk but didn't know her way around so well. She wanted to take us down to the walking trail in the park and around the lake but wasn't sure of the exact turns to take to get back home. But we were. We were able to lead her home; all she had to do was follow us.

The Dog to Human Translation: Know your surroundings. Know your streets, your neighborhood, your neighbors. This way in case something happens and you need to find your way home or tell someone how to get to your house, you can.

Be cautious of strangers.

When someone comes to our door (or just comes in the general area of our home), we bark at them. We let them know that they are entering our territory and they have to get past us first. When we meet someone new in the neighborhood or park, we sniff them to make sure they're ok. If we're near Mom or Dad, we'll check with them to see if the person is ok before heading off to play.

> **The Dog to Human Translation:** Be careful. Be aware when you meet someone new. Check them out (not necessarily by sniffing them); ask questions; get to know them. And for heaven's sake, if someone comes to your door, use the peephole to see whom it is before opening up. If there's any doubt, just don't open the door to your home.

If you see a mess, clean it up.

We do our part to keep our neighborhood clean. When we're out on a walk, Bertram will pick up and bring home empty water bottles or empty paper cups that other people threw away. She's done this since she was a puppy. The first time she did it she was about six months old and we were out for a long walk in the Cuyahoga Valley National Park on a Sunday morning. Right when we were starting out, Bertram found an empty plastic water bottle on the side of the trail. She picked it up and wouldn't let go! Mom and Dad tried to make her give it up, but she refused. She ended up carrying it during the entire walk, even earning a compliment from a Park Ranger on her efforts to clean up the trail. Twelve years later, she's still helping clean up her neighborhood. We've both gotten smart, though. Now, we'll only give up a treasure in exchange for a treat!

The Dog to Human Translation: If you see garbage laying around when you're out and about, pick it up and throw it out. It doesn't matter if it's not yours; we're all stewards of our neighborhoods. Enough said on that one.

Stick to a schedule.

You could set your watch by us. In fact, with the two of us around, we make sure Mom knows exactly what time it is. 10a.m.? Morning stretch and tinkle break. 11a.m.? Walk time. 11:30? We're about ready for lunch. 2p.m.? Afternoon walk. 4:00? Dinner time. 8:00? Bed time. Of course there are exceptions, like if we're out for a car ride or doing something else fun, but if we're home and it's a normal day, that's the schedule. We know what we want, when we want it. We're not happy about too much deviation and will provide helpful reminders every minute or so that it's time to do something specific with us. The reminders will increase in urgency and volume until they catch on.

The Dog to Human Translation: There's some comfort in having a schedule, but it's also healthy to break things up once in a while to keep things from getting dull and boring. But getting into the practice of getting to bed at a certain time or waking up at a certain time can provide consistency and lead to increased mental wellbeing because you're going to be more rested and refreshed. You don't need to keep a schedule that's as rigid as ours, but regular meal times, regular breaks, and rest time will keep you healthy and happy. You'll feel more energized and focused, and be able to be more present in your work and interactions with others.

> *Things like regularly scheduled meals or breaks may be difficult, especially if you find yourself in a "zone" or are engrossed in something, or maybe you just can't seem to find the time. It's important to make the time... you owe it to yourself and to those around you.*

Offer to help with the laundry.

We love to help with the laundry, especially when it's cold outside and Mom opens the dryer door and all the warm air comes out. That's when we're the most helpful at this particular chore. We will climb partway in the dryer and inhale all the good smells, bury our head and shoulders in the warm clothes, and then pick a few things to pull out and roll in so that we smell good, too. Doing this helps gets things nice and smooth. It's a bonus when we can find the dryer sheet to pull out– they're fun to shred! We know Mom appreciates when we help unload the dryer for her.

The Dog to Human Translation: This lesson does not just apply to laundry time. It can be doing the dishes, cleaning the basement, painting a room, or washing the car. But since we are so good at helping with laundry, let's stick to that. If you're at home and someone else is doing the laundry, offer to help. After dinner, offer to clean the dishes. Help change the bed sheets. If you're by yourself, find a way to enjoy these mundane chores. Take a deep breath when folding the warm laundry – there's nothing like that freshly cleaned smell! Dance while washing the dishes. Sing while changing the sheets. Whether you're by yourself or with friends or family, chore time doesn't have to be a chore!

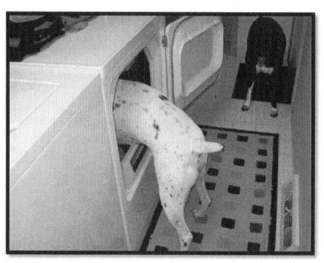

"Helping" with the laundry

Don't put on too much perfume or cologne.

We love good perfume or cologne smells. In fact, we've trained our Mom to keep those paper perfume inserts from magazines in her desk drawer so when we want to smell good, we just sit in front of the drawer and ask (ok, Bertram does that part, but then I join in once she's picked one). When Mom is running low on perfume papers, she calls our Grandma and asks her to send some. A little time later we will get some good smelling mail and it's the mother lode! But back to Mom's desk drawer. After Bertram asks, Mom carefully picks one out, opens the perfume paper up, and we get to rub our necks on it and smell good for the rest of the day. Sometimes we'll try and go back for seconds (because we like it so much), but Mom won't let us. She tells us if we mix perfumes or put too much on, we'll stink. We don't want to stink because that may mean a bath, so we listen to Mom and will go do something else.

> **The Dog to Human Translation:** Don't overdo it on the cologne or perfume. If you want to wear it, put on a spritz and go about your day, just don't put too much on. You don't want to stink. It's pretty simple.

Roll in the cool, shady grass on a hot day (bonus if it's dewy!).

Where we live it gets really hot in the summer so we often have to take our walks early in the morning, before the sun gets too strong. Even then we may have to shorten our adventures. But one thing we do love doing is stopping in the shade of a tree and rolling in the cool grass. We'll run into the shade, slide in on our necks, roll over on our backs, and wiggle back and forth, working our way across the grass. At certain times of the day, Mom will let us play in the shade on the side of our house, and then we get to roll down the hill! What's even better than that? When the grass is covered in dew! It feels so nice and makes us almost giggly! Some mornings it looks like we had a bath, we're so wet! I've sure come a long way since that first trip to the dewy meadow that Mom told you about earlier, huh?

> **The Dog to Human Translation:** This lesson is about really living in the moment. It's a reminder to find that one thing about the situation you're in and turn it around into something positive and enjoyable. Let's take that hot day, for example. When's the last time you laid down in the cool, shady grass on a hot summer day? What about rolling down a hill, like when you were a kid? If laying in the grass is not your thing, what about reading outside on a picnic table under a big tree?

Or going to the park and hiking along a shady trail? Or dipping your toes in the water of a stream? Make the most of the situation you're in – and we don't mean by hiding out in the air conditioning! Get outside and let your creativity find a solution. You can bet the outcome will be something you remember for a longer time than if you binge-watched another TV series.

Post Script from the Pointers

We've been with our Mom and Dad since we were four months old and have been working side-by-side at home with our Mom in her home office for the past eight years. Through all that time, with careful training, we've taught her everything we know. It took a lot of patience and persistence on our part; at times we had to adjust when she just wouldn't catch on. But we endured (we're Pointers, so we're pretty stubborn – or strong-headed, as we like to say) and eventually she would come around.

We spend all day with Mom as she works. We are with her, most days, 24-hours a day. We are her office mates, her companions, her co-workers, her sounding boards. She says we help her keep her sanity through the workday. We listen to her rant when she's upset. We are there when she's brainstorming an idea. We watch her when she's being silly, dancing around the room. We keep her safe during a storm. We are next to her when she exercises, trying to get her attention (successfully thwarting her efforts at a workout). We talk to her all day. When Dad gets home we make sure he sees us first and gives us lots of attention.

When we're not with our Mom or Dad, we keep watch out the window waiting for their return. We wonder if they're ok and can't wait for them to get back home so we're all together. Only then can we truly relax.

We wanted to share everything we've learned so that you can experience the Pointer life. Our hope for you is that you find that same happiness, peace, joy, and contentment after learning these lessons and using them in your life. They are not complicated and don't cost a lot of money. They are simple lessons, but can be complex in their application and most certainly in their results.

We can tell you from our hearts that everything you've read here is true. These are the philosophies that we live by, and they have gotten us everything we could hope for – compassion, love, security, comfort, soft laps, and warm hugs.

And that's more than any dog, or human, could hope for.

Share Your Life Lessons!

We're certain that dogs, and all types of pets for that matter, around the world are teaching their humans life lessons every day, more than we could include here. Do you have a life lesson that you've learned from your own dog, cat, bird, bunny, horse, or other favorite pet? We want to hear about it!

Go to http://petlifelessons.com for expanded stories from Bimmer and Bertram, and to share your lesson. Tell us your story. Don't forget to include where you're from and a picture so we can see who the teacher is! You can also email your lesson to share@petlifelessons.com.

In the meantime, join our Facebook community at http://facebook.com/groups/dogs know best to catch up on the latest from Bimmer and Bertram and also to learn new lessons that others have shared.

We can't wait to hear from you!

Leave a Review for Dogs Know Best

We hope you thoroughly enjoyed reading *Dogs Know Best: Two Dogs' Training Guide for Humans*. We'd appreciate it if you'd head over to Amazon and leave a review so that others will know what to expect when they read it. Thanks in advance for your contribution.

Meet Your Authors

Bimmer & Bertram

Bimmer & Bertram are 12-year-old brother and sister German Shorthaired Pointers born in Akron, Ohio. They had eight siblings, and that meant 10 puppies and two adults living in a tiny bungalow house. They come from a long line of hunters, which explains their strong stalking instinct. They are the best of friends and have never fought or expressed true anger toward each other. They play together, eat together, and watch out for one another, no matter what. You can contact either one through Angie and catch periodic updates about them at
http://petlifelessons.comon
our Facebook Group at
http://facebook.com/groups/dogsknowbest.

Angie

An avid dog lover, Angie Salisbury is the owner of Annibury, LLC (http://annibury.com) and is an entrepreneur, author, and business ghostwriter from Northeast Ohio. Angie is the one who did all the typing. When not focusing her attention on the Pointers – walking the Pointers, feeding the Pointers, playing with the Pointers, petting the Pointers, cleaning up after the Pointers, and generally meeting every conceivable need of the Pointers – she loves being outdoors, reading, getting in a good workout at the gym, or working on her latest intricate needlework piece (possibly another award-winner). She is also a huge fan of puzzles. You can learn more about Angie on her website, at
http://petlifelessons.com,
or by joining our Facebook group at
http://facebook.com/groups/dogsknowbest.

19506393R00062

Made in the USA
Middletown, DE
23 April 2015